The Secret:

How to become a famous actor - in 1 year!

by Stephen Edwards

First edition: 2014

Also available as audiobook.

Foreword

It's a complicated world out there. I know that you don't have time to waste on solving the puzzle in search for your dreams. Because of this, I've decided to give you my exclusive knowledge about show business.

My goal is to have written a complete guide in how to achieve your highest wishes in the business; Becoming a famous actor or actress. Fortunately, I think I might have - so you're in for a real treat.

It's very important that you maximize the absorption of knowledge from this book. Think everything over twice, and don't rush through the pages just to have read it. This is a book written to be very effective and with a high density of valuable facts, so keep in mind to be alert.

Let me tell you one thing before we start; You have to know how to act in order to get the most out of this book. For those who still struggles with techniques and methods, I've written a chapter on acting in order to get you on the right path towards good acting skills. So don't be afraid if you're a newbie, this book is for you.

I want to thank the people who gave me all the valuable knowledge today have in the business. You've all gave me the possibility to write this book. You also gave me the chance to prove myself as an actor and human.

Table of contents

How the industry actually works **8**
How to get famous in a specific country
How to get Hollywood-famous
Why it's difficult to get that big part
How to actually get that big part

Nail the castings - every time **16**
Finding castings - this is how
Networking is a highway
Building your online presence
Preparing for a casting - the best way

Acting - how it's done **29**
Finding your own way of acting
The ultimate practice
Control your emotions - a unique method

Going all in - this is how **35**
Getting a manager, but NOT the wrong one
Why moving to the right city is essential
Flexibility is the key to be loved by casters
How to find yourself surrounded by celebrities
How to avoid being that annoying newbie

The summary **41**
The everyday action you must do, for 1 year
How not to blend in and be a nobody
I saved the best for last; Thinking big is the key

How the industry actually works

'Well, it's not fair - but you can still be Batman'. That summarizes my view on this industry. We all have a chance, but politics is screwing everything up so that you have to fight harder than the son of some sound assistant to one of the Harry Potter movies.

Almost all famous actors have a story. An amazing one. This is what makes it possible for you, wherever you are, whoever you are - to get famous. Even though, you can't sit on a sofa in Germany and think you have a shot at being the next big star in Hollywood. You have to act. And you have to act.

My method for you and your upcoming 365 days is to have a plan. This plan is like a pyramid that you have to climb in order to understand the industry and succeed with the goal of this book.

This industry is as earlier mentioned, built on politics which makes it harder for 'Average Joe' to get that big part. Luckily, we're making our way through that wall of bad odds by understanding how to conquer your geographical location first.

How to get famous in a specific country

In my country of origin, there are is a much bigger chance to get famous compared to USA. This is of course because of the lower amount of citizens, but even in proportion to population - it's easier. The reason is that the country only have a limited amount of "big" and "serious" production companies. This goes for many other countries which is not USA.

If you're finding yourself in a country with limited local productions and a lot of import of foreign sitcoms and movies - you're in a golden spot. The smaller the industry, the bigger the chances.

Whether your goal is to be a famous actor in your home country or the world, the methods of this book applies. Remember to always imagine the different objectives to your own country in order to get a good picture in how you should proceed.

Start out by listing all the big production companies, casting agencies and local TV-channels. Then start finding the web addresses, postal addresses, telephone numbers and names to relevant persons on each company. Look for the directors, casting managers, castings assistants and producers. These persons has the power and interest in casting the best fitting person for the role in their relevant productions.

Then start looking for local websites with ads for castings or being an extra. These websites are perfect in order to get relevant contact information, but also finding new castings.

Start out by trying to apply to as many castings for being an extra as possible. An extra is often hard. Long days, bad salary (if any) and no respect on the set. What you might not know is that many directors are looking for parts for upcoming productions among the extras on a set. This is your *long shot* to get the opportunity to be called to a casting for a big part.

When you're an extra, you might also have the opportunity to get a line or two. This can give you valuable practice in front of a filming crew.

If the luck strikes your path on the set, you might even get upgraded to a small part. Along the way, things during a set can give you opportunities you maybe wouldn't think of. This is why you want to be an extra as much as possible.

The most valuable tip for you when you're going to be an extra is; talk to people. Talk to other extras, talk to people in the filming crew (on breaks, not while working) and talk to the actors. This gives you new contacts that might help you in the future. You have to spread the knowledge about your name and face to as many people as possible. Be sure to introduce yourself in a self-confident way and give a really good first impression.

When applying for different castings, be sure to avoid applying to castings that doesn't fit your profile. Don't apply if you're not fluent in a language they require. Don't apply if you don't have drivers license if that's required. Don't get anyone upset by killing their time. There's not a lot of casting assistants, so be sure to not piss any of them off.

As you might understand; Conquering your home country is all about taking every chance possible. Later, you will learn even more specific tools to get those big castings for big parts in big movies.

Always remember that any chance couldn't be the one. Long shots are often the one that makes the trick. Big parts for big movies aren't just a pure casting of thousands of actors. The actor who got the big part was maybe spotted as an extra in a toothpaste commercial by the sister of a director who happened to see the commercial because she woke an hour too early one morning. It's all about the long shots.

How to get Hollywood-famous

Yes, we have to be realistic. 100% of those who read this book can't get Hollywood-famous. Although, 100% of the readers of this book can increase their chances enormously by following the suggestions of this chapter.

Hollywood is built up by politics. Everybody knows everybody is some kind of weird way and this makes it extremely difficult for an outsider to enter the big Hollywood family.

Therefore, I won't suggest any 'standard' tips like "work hard", "go to many castings" or "practice a lot". Do the exact opposite (kind of...). Let the directors and casting managers want you instead of the opposite. You should not apply to castings. They should call you.

Now you might ask; "How to heck is that possible?". As an answer, I've got two ways to become that person.

1) Stand out.

You do not want to be a good looking twenty-two year old with blonde hair and blue eyes. You will have to compete against five thousand other guys applying for the same part. Also; production companies aren't looking for normal people. Take any movie as an example. How many of the lead characters are normal "Average Joe" people? Not many.

You can stand out by getting special skills or having a special look. Remember the obese guy in 'Lost'? How many obese actors do you think they casted? Well, not as many as boys that were casted as the role of Anakin in Star Wars.

I'm not saying you should gain weight, I'm saying it's positive to have a special look. It could be everything from a naturally lazy eye to being 80 inches tall. Therefore, don't get a teeth whitening, liposuction and a facial just because you're going to Hollywood.

Be yourself. That will increase your chances.

2) ABC (Always be casting).

You might have heard the old sales trick 'Always be closing'. Well, this is my version of "ABC"; Always be casting. By this, I want you to see every moment of the day as an opportunity to be casted.

Be that fun person at the bar doing a Clint Eastwood impression, perform a monologue at the bus station and don't be afraid to show off your skills.

If you have karate skills; show them off at the local karate club where you practice from time to time. One day, a casting assistant may be sent to the karate club in order to find some extras with lines for a movie production. ABC!

Beside these two tips, there's a third. It's about networking, which is discussed later in the book. This third tip is also applicable for those of you eager to make it big in Hollywood.

Be sure to have absorbed these two tips in order to actually turn them into actions. Even though this is just the beginning of this book, one of these tips about might actually be 'the one' that makes you famous. Remember that.

Why it's difficult to get that big part

It's all about the look. New actors often think the casting is a test of how good actors they are. This is 90% wrong. The first casting is always about finding the actors with the perfect look for the part. A good example is children. No child is born with the ability to act, but they all have a unique look. See where I'm going?

So don't be sad because you didn't make it through to the first casting. It's probably because they found someone else looking a lot more like the character than you did. The only exception is if you're a terrible actor, then they might discard from the process you for that reason.

If you're called back to a second casting, be sure to understand the details of the character. More about this in a later chapter.

If you think this through, maybe you can understand why you didn't get certain parts (if you've ever been to a casting). They found someone more suitable looking.

This also takes us back to why a handsome person does not have a greater chance than a non-handsome to get a part. Because it's not about how good you look, it's about how you look.

How to actually get that big part

In order to get a big part, you have to find a big part. This takes us back to an earlier suggestion; list the production companies and casting agencies - but in Hollywood.

With help of services like Imdb Pro and AllMovieCastings.com, you can find all information you need to get in touch with the right people in order to find unlisted castings.

You don't want to disturb anyone in the business, which is why you shouldn't just spam a poor resume and a bad selfie to everyone in Hollywood.

Remember how I earlier said that you shouldn't be the one applying for an casting? Sending out a really good resume and some nice photos of you (not retouched) makes casting assistants wanting to see you if they have a suiting casting. More about this in a later chapter.

Nail the castings - every time

The importance of a good impression at a casting says itself. Even though, many actors and actresses find themselves nervous, unprepared and making a bad impression. So how can I teach you to avoid this?

If you get a script sent to you before a casting, be sure you know the lines inside and out. Now, you may think *"-Of course, what else?"*, which is explainable. Many actors think they've learned the script, even though they haven't. I would say that 3% of all actors at a casting actually knows the script flawless.

To walk that extra mile for a perfect reading of the script. Know every pause, every line and every context you're given. But be sure to not make the most common mistake. Later in this chapter, I will walk you through the mistake and how to avoid it. If you make this mistake, it may cost you a role.

So, what's important besides the tips already given? Well, clothing. If you're not told what to wear, wear a black t-shirt and a pair of jeans or a skirt (in a plain color) - depending what fits your style the best. Don't overdo the perfume, that will just annoy the casting people.

The mentioned tips might seem quite inessential, but the fact is that we want to do a perfect impression in order to get the caster to solely focus on your performance and not the way you're dressed or the way you smell. These are all small but important parts of your full image at the casting.

For the nervous person, it can be a valuable tips to know more about the venue for the casting. *Where is it? How does it look? How do I get there?* The more control you have over the upcoming situation, the more control you have over your nervosity.

Don't try to imagine the casting. No matter how many castings you've been to, you will never figure out how it will be. Things like; "Who will cast me?", "Will I read with someone else?", "Do they have a bathroom?" and "How many people will be there?" is unimportant to think about before the casting.

Focus on practicing the script (if any) or just relax and come unprepared, rested and happy to the casting.

Finding castings - this is how

It's actually easier than you think to find castings. Whether you're looking for castings world wide or locally - there are always many ways to find them. My guess is that the ways you didn't expect would give any castings, will be the ones that actually gives you a part.

Let's start with the most popular ways. On the Internet, there are thousands of websites worldwide that gives you the opportunity to find castings. Start out with finding the local (for your country) and register an account with a complete resume. When this is done, register to the international websites. As an example,

AllMovieCastings.com is a website where you can find international casting calls for free. More often than you think, big production agencies are looking for talents all over the world. Star Wars, Pirates of the Caribbean and The Hunger Games are just a few examples of movies where the casting assistants were looking for extras (and small parts).

Facebook is also a great way to find castings. All over the world, production companies, casting agencies and casting websites are advertising for castings. Like as many pages possible that can give you a casting. Be sure to also look for groups on Facebook. Spend hours and maybe days to just look for all the pages and groups you can find. Be sure to keep yourself updated by constantly reading the ads put out to the pages.

My personal favorite tips to find castings is; ask friends. If you are hired as an extra in a movie or a TV-show, be sure to network amongst the other extras in order to make new friends. Probably, the most of the extras are just like you - trying to make it in the business. They might have great tips for castings that you might not know of. Make many friends and keep each other posted.

When you're at a casting, be sure to make friends with the people waiting for their turn. They can also be a good way to find castings. *"Every person you meet is an opportunity."* Remind yourself of that motto and you will find yourself at a casting one day, thanks to a person you met at a casting or at a job as an extra.

Networking is a highway towards success

As mentioned before; this business is very political. You have to know the right people and hang out at the right places in order to get a casting for a big role in a big production. There are many stories about before unknown "talents" who made a career out of being the star of a big movie. And how do you think they got an audition? Well, they knew someone who knew someone who was working for the casting department. That's a highway towards being called for a casting.

So, what's my point? Change friends? No, not exactly. But expand your network of friends and acquaintances by becoming a real networker. Start going to parties with people in the industry, visit movie premieres, be sure to network in a lunch break when you're an extra, take a class in acting and meet likeminded people. You get my point - try doing everything to a chance to expand your network.

You can read eight books in how to become a networking superstar, but I'll give you my absolutely best tips right here. Probably, you're not a good networker today. No-one are in the beginning of their "networking career".

"Success depends on the support of other people." That's a motto you should read five times slowly, out loud. If you give other people compliments on their work

and achievements - you're easier to like. Nobody likes a person with conversations about themselves, their cats and where they bought their sweater. If you get the chance to network with someone in the business, be sure to be the one asking the questions. That person will feel looked after and interesting - which also make that person more open-minded and open for knowing more about you and your goals.

Listen. *Really listen* to what others have to say. It's hard to like someone who just waits for the other person to stop taking so that they can start their own chatter. If you in a conversation asks follow-up questions and note details in what they're saying, they will feel important and listened on. Every human has a wish to feel important and if you satisfy this feeling, you will be a million times more liked than if you just nod along and starts talking about something else or yourself when the other person has just finished a sentence.

If you're a good networker and attend to many situations where you can practice your skills, this will give you opportunities beyond your wildest dreams. I'm not exaggerating, this will probably give you amazing opportunities. I've got everything from personal experiences to stories told to me about how networking has changed the way of a (sometimes non-existing) career - in a positive way.

People are more accessible than you might think. If you want to get in touch with the casting director of a movie, you're probably just a search on Google and two phone calls away. If you through your networking have information about an ongoing casting where you would fit perfect, just use the force of Internet to get in touch with the right people. Be sure to not be to needy - just drop your resume elegantly in a simple email and hope for the best.

If you're thinking about hiring someone to teach you acting in a more professional way, choose someone you think have a good network. If you practice closely with a tutor, that person might recommend you to people in his/hers network that can give you a unique opportunity. Also, be sure to become good friends and use your networking skills to be a really likable person in the mind of your tutor. Those private lessons in acting can pay off really good in the future if you handle things correctly.

Building your online presence

As you might understand, it's important to have a good online presence. The most people working with casting is looking for prospects all around the Internet, the first one being the local audition ads website.

I earlier mentioned that it's important to create a good profile and resume on these local audition ads websites. But there's also many ways you can make it become more lucrative and visible, because you don't want to just be one in the crowd.

By completing your profile in all kinds of ways, you will be approached to as much more serious than the ones leaving out telephone number, website and of course - good head shots.

I now leave you the task to go to any local audition ads website and fill out your profile to be one hundred percent complete. Avoid grammar mistakes and unnecessary blunders. I trust you to not need any more explanation since the task only need gumption, which I hope you've got.

Online presence isn't only about this, there's many other ways to become more visible which increases your chances in this world full of aspiring actors. This takes us to our next subject, which is; your own website.

The impression of an actor with his or hers own website will be much better since it gives the feeling of seriousness and solemnity. It doesn't matter if you don't have a track record or good acting education - a website with some great shots of you.

Creating your own website might sound difficult, but it's just a matter of ten dollars and a couple of hours work. The website AllMovieCastings.com has a complete tutorial on how to technically set up your own actors website, so I will briefly explain what steps needs to be done;

1. **Buy a domain**.

Typically, your full name dot com. For example: *BradleyCooper.com* if 'Bradley Cooper' was your name. If the domain is taken, just find another top domain such as '.net' or '.info'. If your country has a local TLD (which is most likely), be sure to also register your full name dot local TLD. Maria Litto was a german actress, so her domain would be *MariaLitto.de* since '.de' is the local TLD.

2. **Set up the website.**
   Probably the most fun part of it, since you have to use your creativity in order to find a good looking template for your website. You don't have to worry, it's really easy.
3. **Publish.**
   After a couple of hours of fun work, it's done and you can publish the website. Be sure to link to your new website from all your online profiles, resumes and other relevant places. Remember; ABC!

This is not it. Luckily, there are many more ways to build your online presence. Something to remember before moving on is to always be sure to have the same information everywhere. If you move, change the address on your different resumes and your website immediately.

Two websites I've earlier mentioned is **IMDb** and **AllMovieCastings.com**. These two websites also gives you the possibility to create a profile, visible to anyone. By doing this, you expand your online presence to be even wider. IMDb is the biggest movie and actor database in the world and AllMovieCastings is the best directory for big castings all around the world.

If you're on a budget, it's not necessary to pay for the "premium plans" or whatever offered. The most important task for yourself is to get listed. If you have the money to spare, then use it to get a paid profile - which probably gives you a better visibility and the possibility to add pictures.

As a way to connect your website and your different online resume pages, it's good to have a Facebook page, Twitter account and Instagram account. The Facebook page is a good platform to add all the great photos of you on set. Also, the images you took for your resume can be posted. By doing this, a Google search on your name will give a more relevant result, given your name is fairly unique.

Twitter is a great channel for meeting other aspiring actors. Spend some hours on following all the people in the same situation as you. Also, follow all the nearby casting agencies, production companies and casting directors. In this way, you'll get a good overview of the current productions and a great way to getting to know "the right people" online. Spend half an hour everyday on Twitter; tweeting, retweeting and reading tweets. Solely this tips is super valuable for a person like you, looking for jobs and contacts. Don't just keep reading and think "-Yea, I'll do that". Put down the book and create an account on Twitter for your acting profile. Pick a username such as ”FirstnameLastname_Actor” or similar. In this way, you’re easily identified.

In order to save time when publishing; add a connection for auto posts from Instagram to Twitter (IFTTT.com). Then enable auto posting from Twitter to Facebook. By doing this, you only have to publish material on Instagram - the rest is solved by auto posting. Except for of course; the network building tweets.

Preparing for a casting - the best way

There are a thousand ways to prepare for a casting ”the best way” and this is my version of it. I base my version on the memoirs and biographies of great actors who’ve written about their best career tips.

If you received a script to practice on, prior to the casting - read it. Read it a thousand times. As I’ve said before, it’s extremely important to really know the script. But! And this is a big but; Do not practice feelings.

What do I mean by this? Well, feelings ”in real life” are spontaneous - so why rehearse a feeling which should present itself naturally in the casting? If you were to read the script with a friend - with feelings, your brain would automatically learn and record those feelings. When the casting comes, all the feelings you’ve subconsciously recorded will appear and it’ll feel unnatural.

The casting people are experts in reading feelings and emotions - so don’t try to trick them. Instead, try to only practice the actual lines and when you read them out loud, practicing at home, do it without emotions or visualizing the scenario. Use a monotone and flat voice in order to avoid recording feelings.

Instead, react naturally in the dialogue. Be focused by transforming to the character and feel what the character feels. It's easier than you think. That's why improve is easier for beginners in acting; because the lines comes spontaneous and feelings appear naturally.

If you're not given a script prior to the casting, just relax. The point of going to a casting without given material is up to you to embrace. Don't start thinking about what you're going to do, who you are going to meet and irrelevant thoughts that just blocks you from action and thinking clear. Just accept the fact that you're going to a casting to show yourself, probably tell them something about you before a camera and then maybe answer some easy personal questions.

If you're not experienced in going to castings today, I'll give you some hints about how it might look like, who you're going to meet and how a casting process is done.

The casting process

A casting agency or a production company with a casting team as employees is given the mission to cast people for a production. The director might give the casting team an insight in how the characters should look like and how they will behave. Based on this, a costume designer might also start working parallel with choosing the outfits for the cast - but it also depends on the final look of the casted actors.

The casting team puts out advertisement in order to get actors to search. In one case, the casting team might put out advertisement all over a country (or the world) in search for the right cast. Many big movies were casted this way. The upside is all the thousands of faces to choose from. The downside is that the skills in acting is in average low amongst the searching.

In an other case, a casting team might just give some actors a call in order to get them to cast. In these cases, we're talking about well-known professional actors. This is the scenario of Hollywood top movies today. You don't see a new aspiring actor in the latest romantic comedy with a hundred million dollar budget.

The casting

I'm going to give you the *regular* scenario of a casting. This is maybe not how your next casting will look like, but the odds are it's very similar.

As you approach the casting building, there will be some signs in order to avoid people getting lost. Be sure to look for these, because you don't want to disturb the casting team who are busy casting.

When you enter the building/room, there will be someone welcoming you and giving you a form to fill out.

The form will be some personal questions (name, gender, postal address, email address, telephone number, height and other relevant facts). There might already in this scenario be a contract to sign, containing information about the salary, location and other relevant conditions. This is to ”have that part done” if you’re casted.

After that, you’re most probably up for some head shots and full body shots in front of a camera. This is to get up to date pictures of all casted, also with the same lightning.

Then we have the wait until you’re up. After this, it’s very different - but I’ll give you a hint. The casting person will give you the scenario before the camera starts recording. You’ll be able to ask some questions. Also, another actor might be in the room since you’re probably going to read a script with someone.

After the casting, you’ll be given the information that they’ll get in touch if you’re welcome back for the second casting (if there is any). In ”serious” productions, there’s always a process of three castings (if you go all the way). First, one with the casting team. Second, another with the casting team (but longer and with more context and scenarios). Thirdly, one with the actual director.

Acting - how it's done

This is not a book about the art of acting. I will not teach you techniques for acting. This book is about how to reach to the top in the business. But, I can't resist giving you some basic tips, like the one in the previous chapter about how to not "record emotions" while practicing a script.

There are many fantastic books about methods and techniques of acting. Therefore, I leave this part up to these books. Why re-invent the wheel? You can find some of these tips at AllMovieCastings.com/books.

A book is a great way to learn, but as earlier mentioned - a private teacher is the optimal (and unfortunately the most expensive) way. Depending on which country you live in, the market for personal acting teacher might be either good or bad. If you're looking for making it big by moving to Los Angeles, you may find the best ones with the best networking potential.

There are also classes all around the world - in acting. The quality of many of these classes can be discussed, but if you see a class with good testimonials and interesting learning plan - why not jump aboard?

Of course, there's also the universities with highly professional acting educations. In some countries (such as Sweden), these educations are free and in other (such as United States), they cost.

Depending on what you think is the best for you, choose the way to educate yourself if you haven't done that yet. You have everything from a book to a five year education to choose from. And hey, just do it! Life is to short to "wait for the right time".

Finding your own way of acting

I've learned something very valuable and I want you to embrace this knowledge. Find your own way of acting, when you've gotten the hang of it. It's not natural following techniques your whole career and "everybody" learns this after a couple of years of professional acting. Your own modified techniques, guidelines and ways of acting are the best for you.

From my personal and professional perspective, acting isn't something you learn - it's just something you do. Every time a person is lying, that person is acting. When a person is telling you an anecdote, that person is acting (a little). We all act sometimes without thinking about it, which also makes it easier. Assume I said this to a person: *"- Hey, every time you tell a lie, you're acting because you're fabricating feelings and improvising information."* I think that person would be worse at lying after that. Conclusion: Don't think you're acting - just act.

But, we can go even further. Every time a person is angry, that person is doing exactly what you should do when you're on a set. Acting. An event of incidents and conversation has led to an angry person. Why is this person angry? Well, because it's the natural way of reaction for that person after that event of incidents.

By just reacting in the most natural way in a scene, you're far up on the ladder of acting skills. Don't think "oh, is this where I get angry?" - just *get* angry. When shooting a movie (or other production), you might not always get the context you want. *As an example: In the most cases, you're going to start off without the previous line from another actor - which gives you the mission to start acting from zero. Because of this, it's important to sink into the scene before the director shouts "action!".* Theatre actors don't have this problem since a theatre is non-stop.

Remember the importance of finding your own way of acting. I've given you some hints, but I want you to proceed in finding your path. What's your technique? How is your way of sinking in to your character on the first day of a production? Trust yourself, no matter what.

The ultimate practice

By acting every day, you keep yourself in control of your feelings constantly. The practice you need to be a ninja at doing difficult scenes such as crying on demand takes time and consistency is the key when you're aiming to be really good at something.

You can easily find the scripts for almost all famous movies online, which makes it possible for you to practice everything from learning a script to acting it (preferably with an actor friend). This is a great way to practice since it's also a lot of fun to act out roles from your favorite Hollywood movies.

Control your emotions - a unique method

Firstly, you have to be secure in yourself. Self-confidence is highly important to have in order to act. Before moving on to this technique, I will give you my thoughts on self-confidence and how you get passed that block that limits you in your everyday life. You only have to read this if you feel that you've got issues with anything from speaking before a crowd to blushing.

When a person lacks self-confidence, that's because that person is afraid of what people might think of him (or her, but I will use "him" in my example). This is a bad loop since people have the tendency to think less good about a shy and quiet person compared to a self-confident, social person.

If he is so afraid of what people might think of him, why doesn't he give them a good impression instead of standing there, shy and quiet? A change is vital in order to get out of this bad loop.

The first impression is the most important. This is because if a shy person suddenly one day is the most self-confident person in the world - that's strange and it all backfires. But when you're going to a casting, you have the possibility in making the best 'first impression' ever made.

Everything a person knows about another person is from the impressions they've gotten throughout all the meetings the person have had with the other. If a person deep inside still is shy, even though the ”outside” is self-confident, no-one who meets him for the first time will know. This is a comforting thought that should help you get out of the loop.

Be confident, speak loud, hold you head up high, have a straight back, make eye-contact and say hello to everyone with a big smile. This is how you make a good first impression. As a bonus, when you've done this very self-confident first impression, everything will be so much easier. Other people will treat you as a person with good confidence, which also will make you feel like you have it. This is a good loop that will result in an overall better confidence.

Now, when your confidence is good and you have no trouble controlling your emotions - it's time to use it in acting. As earlier mentioned, it's very important to not practice scripts with emotions. I would say none at all, but it's up to you to decide what's best in your case.

By arriving to a set with the script flawlessly learned, you have a great chance to really show your characters true emotions in the scenes.

Think about it this way: You've learned the script, so the lines are in the back of your head. But don't think about them. <u>React naturally in the dialogue, but use the words of the script.</u>

Not many amateur actors thinks about it this way at all, which also makes many actors mediocre in their performance. I think the underlined part is so important that you should make it your screensaver, smartphone background and that you should write it on a paper - always in your pocket, there to remind you. Let's hear it again; React naturally in the dialogue, but use the words of the script.

Going all in - this is how

Determination is vital. Doing something with 80% of your energy will not give you results. Doing something giving 200% of your energy will give you results, guaranteed. So why waste your time giving almost everything, when you can give everything you've got (and a little more)?

There are numerous actions for going all in and I hope you'll embrace them and actually convert my tips into actions. For the sake of your career, do as many actions as possible. You have to take the big step out into the unknown and risky in order to gain the ultimate goal. As a wise person once said; *"Taking risks are risky. But not taking any risks at all is even more risky."*

Getting a manager - but NOT the wrong one

I know what you're thinking; "- What? A manager?! But I'm barely an actor?". Don't worry, you're not getting the kind of manager you first might think of. A manager for a professional actor have the job to sort by the offers given. The manager I'm talking about is the one looking for castings.

Unfortunately, there's a lot of people out there looking for peoples money. Companies or persons offering 'managers for actors' is often this kind of fraud, if you're at the wrong place. This is why I'm going to give you the tips for a fool proof manager, the one you can always trust and who doesn't cost you a fortune.

If you're going all in, everybody in your presence (family and friends) should know it. Some people will support you and some people (with unhealthy thinking patterns) will think you're a fool that even gives it a try.

After a while of going to castings and doing your best, you'll notice what people in your surrounding that have a genuine interest in what you do. They often ask how things are going and shows a true interest when you're telling them. These people (or this person) are unique in the way they think. Just like you, they think that anything is possible and this is the kind of person we like.

If you identify this person in your surrounding that you also are comfortable with - you should give them the opportunity to be your manager. The role as a manager will be to search for castings in all those areas that it's relevant and to network in your behalf. This is because you want to save time so that you together can search for even more castings, but also so that you can get time over to practice on your acting. The manager could even handle your social media accounts if you feel that's relevant and effective. The most important thing is that the person who takes the role as your manager is driven, gives you support, pep talks prior to castings and has a good flow when searching for castings.

Another version is that you meet someone passionate on the set of a production. When networking on the set, as previously taught, you might 'click' very good with, let's say one of the sound technician. If that person really likes the idea, that person (and now; manager) also comes with a network of people in the business.

It's hard to make it without the support of others, and what is more efficient than a manager, constantly making progress for you and support you when you're in a bad mood.

Why moving to the right city is essential

One thing isn't fair and that's what city you should live in versus the city you actually live in. Depending on what country you're living in, there's almost always the capital of the country or some other city in the country that's optimal to live in as an actor since all the productions and castings are made there.

Los Angeles (United States) is probably one of the world's most relevant places to live in order to find castings. If you're living in the ninth biggest city in Germany, you should probably move to Berlin. You know best when it comes to what city you should live in, in your country. And if that's not the city you're living in now; move.

I know, it's hard. You have to move away from family and friends and probably get a more expensive place to live. But if you're going to make it, you have to move. Living in the city where it all happens is such an important factor that it's non discussable. There's no short cut, just do it. But change is positive and you'll find new friends. See the positive things with moving, instead if focusing on the downside.

Flexibility is the key to be loved by casters

If you live in the city 'where it all happens', you're probably going to be very flexible. In this way, you don't have to check flights and ask the caster to call back later, which is something that might lead to a missed opportunity.

Flexibility also includes coming in on short notice. If you've went to a casting and haven't received any response afterwards, you're probably out. What you might not know is that you're the backup plan. If you were second best (which you'll probably never know), that means; you're the one to call if the casted actor drop off. Since a movie production includes so many people and so much planning - a drop off can't slow things down or change the plans of anything.

If someone in the casting team calls you up and asks for something, just go with it. It can be everything from dressing up in a suit to come on fifteen minutes notice. Casting people are stressed people and if you're flexible, they'll love you.

How to find yourself surrounded by celebrities

To have a good network is, as earlier mentioned, a key towards success on a high level. By having a good network, you will be invited to various parties, premieres and other get-togethers. Always visit these when you're invited, because you never know what persons will attend. When you're mingling around, getting to know people, someone might introduce you to a friend of theirs. That friend can be anybody. And I mean, anybody.

The show business is very political and this is why you have to use a lot of time and energy on networking. If you're that nice, self-confident person on all the parties and mingles amongst the people in the business - people will start recommending you to others. Be open with what you do (acting) and that you're constantly looking for new opportunities.

Invest in a good suit or dress, some really fresh casual clothes and bring your best smile to all the parties you're attending. Always be in your best mood with your best clothes and you'll shine with positive energy and good vibes.

Be sure to know the latest in the business prior going to a party. In this way, you can join more conversations and even deliver some new information, which makes you more interesting and therefore desirable in a conversation.

How to avoid being that annoying newbie

Be transparent and don't act like you're something you're not - that's my first advise. Nobody likes a pretentious amateur. I promise you; someday you will meet that pretentious amateur and know what I mean. That guy who were "*Guy on bus #8*" in the latest blockbuster and thinks he rules the world. Don't be friends with people like him and do everything you can to avoid becoming like him.

An effective way to get more attention and likability amongst people is to listen really close to what they're saying in a conversion. Don't just say "*yea*" and "*aha*" when a person is telling a story. Ask follow-up questions, show your emotions more than normal and look the person in the eyes when he talks. In this way, you give a really good impression and that person will feel listened on and will therefore listen better when you talk or ask for a favor.

When people asks what you're doing and you tell them you're an actor, be transparent with your goals and what professional jobs you've done as an actor (if any). Don't leave it up to them to visualize how successful or unsuccessful you are - tell them right away. Transparency is honesty and honesty is good - everybody likes an honest person.

The summary

This book has a lot of information, tips and paths. It's up to you to choose which of these you actually want to do. If you want to be a professional actor within the shortest time possible, you have to embrace as many as these tips as possible. But there are some tips I've saved for last, because they're are the most important ones.

The everyday action you must do, for 1 year

It can be hard to work and fight towards a goal every day of every week of every month of every year - but it's gold. In order to get something done every day, I've put together a scheme containing all those things you should do every day. Print it and put it over your bed, on your fridge and on your smartphone.

- **Twitter networking**
  Follow some new people, retweet good tweets and tweet some good Youtube video related to acting or other relevant information that your followers might like.

- **Instagram and Facebook status updating**
  Because nobody likes a Facebook page or Instagram account that updates seldom.

- **Look for castings**
  Spend hours on looking for new castings.

- **Practice acting**
  It's both fun and necessary.

- **If you have a script to learn; practice**
  Don't underestimate the time needed to do this.

- **Look for parties or premieres you can attend**
  Because if you've learned something in this book, it's that networking is the highway.

- **Exercise**
  Your mind and body needs regular exercise. Go to the gym or practice your favorite sport. In the stressful environment of castings, the body needs to exercise.

With this list of actions, every day will take you closer to a break-through. Doing something every day for your career is like fast forwarding your career. Other people don't have the energy, but you have because you know how close you actually are to your goals.

How not to blend in and be a nobody

If you were to see a pink car with clowns in it driving in the street - you would remember that for a pretty long time. What about all those other thousands of cars you saw the same day - do you remember them? That black Volvo? No, of course not. The psychology behind this phenomena will give you an advantage.

Now, it's up to you to think. You have to start thinking outside the box, all the time. When you're going to a casting; what can you do that's unique and special, so that they remember you? I don't want you to dress up in pink clothes (even though that would work). I just want you to go the extra mile and do something no-one else done during the whole casting process. Preferably something that shows how self-confident, skilled or likable you are.

I'm going to give you one fun tips that I heard some actor did in the waiting room outside a casting, waiting for his turn. He faked a really awkward phone call which made him show a lot of different emotions and a long improvised dialogue with no-one on the other end of the phone. The casting team who sat on the other end of the room, sorting papers, overheard the whole phone call and thought it was awkward to even be in the same room as him - because of the explicit content of the dialogue. When he "hang up", he waited for any reactions in the room, but it was dead quiet. Then he asked; *"- So, what did you think?"*. The people in the room bursted out in laughter and the success was a fact. Now, that's how you avoid blending in.

A whole different way of avoid blending in is to acquire some unique skills. I have a friend who got himself a pilots license in order to have something special on his actor resume. Many well-known actors actually have special skills, such as karate, shooting, piloting, diving, singing or dancing. So, why not invest in some singing lessons or karate classes? If the times come when a casting team have to choose between you and one other actor, it can be crucial with that special skill that's needed for the part. Otherwise, they would have to teach the other actor - which would take both time and money.

If you have a passion for dancing and one of your biggest dreams is to play a character in a dance inspired movie, then take all the classes needed - because one day, you'll live that dream.

I saved the best for last; Thinking big is the key

A person who thinks it's impossible to become the president of United States is a person who lack the knowledge in thinking big. The world is full of people who lack this way of thinking and that makes them mediocre people with mediocre jobs and mediocre lives where they didn't achieved their dreams.

By thinking big and dreaming big, you will live big and achieving big. Since you read this book, I don't think you have problem with thinking big since you are open to the possibility that you within a short amount of time will be a successful actor. Although, the magnitude of thinking big is still a variable.

Nobody became successful by incident, it's all in their minds. If you set your mind to it, you will live your dreams some day. It's not discussable, you will guaranteed achieve your goals as long as you are determined.

A person who've identified his goals and is willing to go all in, that's a person who will succeed. It's not about having time or having money to do it - it's about knowing it's possible and that it's going to be done. If you can't afford quitting your job in order to focus on acting, you'll find a way to afford if you just think big.

Don't think like average Joe, think different and think big. Average Joe has the word "impossible" in his vocabulary, but that's a word you'll never use - because you think big. Anything is possible and that's your power.

6979470R00029

Printed in Great Britain
by Amazon.co.uk, Ltd.,
Marston Gate.